Emteaz H

Blood

Bloomsbury Methuen Drama
An imprint of Bloomsbury Publishing Plc

B L O O M S B U R Y
LONDON • NEW DELHI • NEW YORK • SYDNEY

Bloomsbury Methuen Drama
An imprint of Bloomsbury Publishing Plc
www.bloomsbury.com

50 Bedford Square
London
WC1B 3DP
UK

175 Fifth Avenue
New York
NY 10010
USA

BLOOMSBURY, METHUEN DRAMA and the Diana logo
are trademarks of Bloomsbury Publishing Plc

First published 2015

British Library Cataloguing-in-Publication Data
A catalogue record for this book is available from the British Library

ISBN: PB: 978-1-4742-5079-5
ePub: 978-1-4742-5080-1
ePDF: 978-1-4742-5081-8

Library of Congress Cataloging-in-Publication Data
A catalog record for this book is available from the Library of Congress

Typeset by Country Setting, Kingsdown, Kent CT14 8ES
Printed and bound in Great Britain

Tamasha and The Belgrade Theatre present

Blood

by Emteaz Hussain

Directed by Esther Richardson

Esmée Fairbairn
FOUNDATION

LOTTERY FUNDED

Supported using public funding by
ARTS COUNCIL
ENGLAND

Cast

Caneze	**Krupa Pattani**
Sully	**Adam Samuel-Bal**

Creative Team

Writer	**Emteaz Hussain**
Director and Dramaturg	**Esther Richardson**
Designer	**Sara Perks**
Lighting Designer	**Aideen Malone**
Composer/Sound Designer	**Arun Ghosh**
Movement Director	**Kitty Winter**

Production Team

Production Manager	**Dennis Charles**
Technical Stage Manager	**Laura Stevens**
Company Stage Manager	**Jane Andrews**
Stage Manager (tour cover)	**Andy Shewan**
Press Consultant	**Kate Morley PR**
Publicity photography	**Sophia Schorr-Kon**
Promotional Video	**Nye Williams** and **Clare Callen**
Production Photography	**Robert Day**

Tamasha Developing Artists

Assistant Director	**Ryan Harston**
Observer	**Christa Harris**

Thank You

Tamasha would like to thank: all the team at the Belgrade Theatre;
Quantrina Hussain; Miggy Angel; Nadine Rennie; Philip Osment,
Suba Das, Taj Atwal, Asif Khan, the Grimsby Telegraph,
and all the performers and creative teams involved in the previous
R&Ds and showcases including Propeller at the Gate in 2008 and
at the Curve in 2013; New Wolsey Theatre; and everyone else
who has contributed to the project.

Belgrade Theatre, Coventry

The Belgrade Theatre was built in 1958 as part of the reconstruction of Coventry after World War II. Holding 858 in our two-tier main auditorium, and 250 in the flexible, second space, B2, we remain one of the largest regional producing theatres in Britain.

Autumn 2007 saw the re-opening of the Belgrade Theatre after completion of our £14 million redevelopment project, including the creation of B2, and refurbishment of the existing listed building.

Having invented the Theatre-in-Education (TiE) movement in the 1960s, we continue to pioneer new initiatives in this field as well as other community and outreach programmes.

The theatre remains the major arts and cultural facility in Coventry and the only building-based professional producing theatre company in the city. We present a broad spectrum of excellent work and co-produce a wide range of shows to appeal to and grow diverse audiences

Recent Belgrade productions include: *The Alchemist*, The Spanish Golden Age Season, *Three Minute Heroes*, UK premieres of *Propaganda Swing* and *Only a Day* as well as our annual pantomime and alternative B2 Christmas Show.

Website: **www.belgrade.co.uk**

Box Office: **024 7655 3055**

@BelgradeTheatre

www.facebook.co.uk/BelgradeTheatreCoventry

Belgrade Management Team

Artistic Director	**Hamish Glen**
Executive Director	**Joanna Reid**
Chairman of the Board of Directors	**Stewart Fergusson**
Director of Production	**Adrian Sweeney**
Director of Communications	**Nicola Young**
Communications Manager	**Ray Clenshaw**
Associate Director, Community & Education	**Justine Themen**
General Manager	**Claire Simpson**
Commercial Director	**David Jane**
Financial Controller	**David Caldwell**

'Tamasha is a mirror reflecting a nation of continuing change and creativity, of mixings and mergings. British culture needs reminding it has always been global. Tamasha's stirring, audacious work makes sure the nation never forgets what it is.'

tamasha

Yasmin Alibhai-Brown, cultural commentator

Tamasha is Britain's foremost touring theatre company producing new plays inspired by the diversity of a globalised world. Our work places the voices of emerging and established artists from culturally diverse backgrounds centre-stage.

Our approach is boldly investigative and located along 'cultural fault lines', leading the debate around the meeting points and multiple narratives of contemporary Britain and beyond. We:

- present new plays from seldom-heard voices, charting the reality of lived multiculturalism

- train theatre artists and young people through 'Tamasha Developing Artists'

- facilitate theatremakers to engage creatively with communities and audiences

'Tamasha opened up an industry which previously felt closed to me. I am now a professional dramatist – all because of Tamasha's amazing work nurturing talent from diverse communities.'   Ishy Din, writer of *Snookered*

'Tamasha means commotion, creating a stir, and the company is certainly doing that.'
What's On Stage on *Snookered*

www.tamasha.org.uk

Support Us
A launchpad for creative careers

'Tamasha work tirelessly to find and develop new diverse talent for the theatre. I have seen many actors and writers progress significantly with their guidance and support. Tamasha is living proof that great creative work and diversity go hand in hand.'
Lorraine Heggessey, Executive Chair, Boom Pictures (Ex-Controller BBC1)

Tamasha has been creating a stir on the British stage for 25 years. We have a proud history of changing lives, propelling unknown talent into tomorrow's leading artists. We have launched the careers of many well-known artists such as Parminder Nagra (*Bend it Like Beckham*), Jimi Mistry (*West is West*) and Raza Jaffrey (*Spooks*), and we continue to nurture the next generation through the Tamasha Developing Artists (TDA) programme.

Become a Tamasha supporter and be part of:

* finding and supporting the next generation of diverse UK actors, writers and directors to sustain their own careers

* propelling artists from under-represented backgrounds into the mainstream

* supporting innovative ideas from a seed through to production

* giving creative opportunities to young people whose backgrounds may not always encourage it

You can make a tangible difference. The money you give will go directly towards nurturing emerging artists and uncovering the next generation of unheard voices. Help us to continue to shape the cultural landscape, and ensure that stories on the stage truly reflect Britain as it is today.

To find out more about these opportunities and unique benefits, please contact Sudha on friends@tamasha.org.uk or 020 7749 0090.

Tamasha gratefully acknowledges financial support from Esmée Fairbairn Foundation, the Garrick Charitable Trust and the Friends and Patrons of Tamasha.

Tamasha Friends and Patrons

Anant Shah (President of the Friends), Aarti Bhanderi, Matt Carter, Milan & Gita Chauhan, Régis Cochefert, Shernaz Engineer, Stella & Daniel Flowers, Mukesh & Kundan Gohil, GV Films Limited, aad Haafiz, Mobeen Jassat, Azam Javaid & Shayasta Ashiq, Bir & Gerlinde Kathuria, Shaheen Khan, Jay Lakhani, Zachary Latif, Nilesh and Nina Majeethia, Luke Mason, Sarah Moorehead, Salil Patankar & Mrs Patankar, Daksha Patel, Lopa Patel, Sanjiv Patel, Shiv & Reena Popat, Brett & Lisa Sainty, Nitin Shah, Anshu Srivastava, Ramesh & Ella Vala, Alan, Linda & Ana Westall together with those who wish to remain anonymous.

SOHO THEATRE

London's most vibrant venue for theatre, comedy and cabaret.

Soho Theatre is a major creator of new theatre, comedy and cabaret. Across our three different spaces we curate the finest live performance we can discover, develop and nurture. Soho Theatre works with theatre makers and companies in a variety of ways, from full producing of new plays, to co-producing new work, working with associate artists and presenting the best new emerging theatre companies that we can find. We have numerous writers and theatre makers on attachment and under commission, six young writers and comedy groups, and we read and see hundreds of shows a year – all in an effort to bring our audience work that amazes, moves and inspires.

'Soho Theatre was buzzing, and there were queues all over the building as audiences waited to go into one or other of the venue's spaces. [The audience] is so young, exuberant and clearly anticipating a good time.' Guardian

We attract over 170,000 audience members a year.

We produced, co-produced or staged over forty new plays in the last twelve months.

Our social enterprise business model means that we maximise value from Arts Council and philanthropic funding; we actually contribute more to government in tax and NI than we receive in public funding.

sohotheatre.com
Keep up to date: **sohotheatre.com/mailing-list**
 **facebook.com/sohotheatre**
 **twitter.com/sohotheatre**
 **youtube.com/sohotheatre**

Supported using public funding by
ARTS COUNCIL ENGLAND
LOTTERY FUNDED

Creative Team

EMTEAZ HUSSAIN | Writer

Emteaz is a performance poet, playwright and workshop leader. Her acclaimed first play *Sweet Cider* was produced by Tamasha in 2008 following her outstanding work through the Tamasha Developing Artists (TDA) programme's New Writing Course. *Blood* was originally performed in 2010 at the Gate Theatre as part of Tamasha's new writing showcase, Propeller. She is currently commissioned by Pilot Theatre and Clean Break, and is on assignment to the Royal Court Theatre, London. As a spoken word artist she has performed nationally and internationally and has toured, in the past, with Transglobal Underground, Fundamental, Hustlers HC and as a backing poet with the Benjamin Zephaniah band. Emteaz works extensively as a workshop practitioner in both statutory and community settings, specialising in Pupil Referral Units.

ESTHER RICHARDSON | Director and Dramaturg

Esther is a freelance theatre and film director. She has worked as an Associate for Soho Theatre, Derby LIVE and CAST in Doncaster. She founded the new writing company Theatre Writing Partnership which ran for ten years in Nottingham. Her varied work as a director includes productions for Nottingham Playhouse, Derby LIVE, Royal & Derngate, Northampton, Soho Theatre and Octagon Theatre, Bolton. Her film work includes two short films, one of which, *The Cake*, was chosen as the UK film for the Women in Film in Television International Showcase and was screened all over the world in 2012. She was also one of eight emerging film directors to be selected for Creative England's prestigious iFeatures2 feature film development scheme in 2012.

SARA PERKS | Designer

Sara has designed over 140 productions for a wide variety of theatres, venues, sites and genres. *Betty Blue Eyes* toured nationally last year, and other notable designs include *Spring Storm* and *Beyond the Horizon* (National Theatre and Royal & Derngate, Northampton,); *King and I* (national tour & Curve, Leicester); *Gypsy, Hello Dolly!* and *Hotstuff* (Curve, Leicester); *The Glee Club* (CAST, Doncaster); *Depot* (a multi-discipline promenade site-specific piece); *Saturday Night and Sunday Morning, Journey's End* (Mercury Theatre, Colchester); *Return to the Forbidden Planet* (tour); *Forgotten Things* and *Ugly* (Red Ladder); *Elixir of Love* (co-design, Grange Park Opera); Neil LaBute's *Helter Skelter/Land of the Dead/The Furies* (touring for Bush Theatre and Dialogue); *Union Street* (Plymouth Theatre Royal's millennium project with a cast of over 230). She also designed the original production of the cult musical *Saucy Jack and the Space*

Vixens. She has been Associate Designer at the Mercury Theatre, Colchester, and English Touring Theatre (designs included *Eden End*, *Romeo and Juliet*) and holds an Edinburgh Fringe First, the John Elvery Theatre Design Award and a Vision Design (Costume) Award from the BBC. She works with and for students at LAMDA, RADA, Mountview, Arts Ed and Central School of Speech and Drama. saraperkstheatredesign.co.uk

AIDEEN MALONE | Lighting Designer

Aideen trained in drama and theatre in Trinity College Dublin and Goldsmiths University of London. Over the past twenty years she has worked extensively in theatre, dance and opera. She works regularly with Turtle Keys Arts creating designs for Red Cape, Flying Cloud, Joli Vyann, Smith Dance Theatre, Angika and Arc Dance. She has worked with English Touring Opera on many productions. With Akram Khan she has created the lighting design for *Kaash*, *Related Rocks* and *Polaroid Feet*. She has collaborated with Jude Kelly and Paco Peña on *Quimeras* and *A Compas*. With Sally Cookson she has created the lighting design for *Hetty Feather* and *Romeo and Juliet* and also for *Jane Eyre* at Bristol Old Vic, which will be showing at the National Theatre in 2015. With Sadhana Dance she has created designs for *The Shiver*, *Elixir* and *Under My Skin*. Aideen has been a lighting design tutor at ALRA for many years. She is also a director of Junction, which designs lighting sculptures and installations.

ARUN GHOSH | Composer/Sound Designer

Arun Ghosh is a British-Asian clarinettist, composer and musical director. He has released three critically acclaimed albums, *Northern Namaste*, *Primal Odyssey* and *A South Asian Suite*, on camoci records. Other significant works in his repertoire include his re-score of feature-length animation *The Adventures of Prince Achmed*, contemporary dance work *A Handful of Dust* and programme symphony, *Spitalfields Suite*. A key player on the UK jazz scene, Ghosh is a renowned innovator of the Indo-Jazz style, and has appeared on the cover of *Jazzwise* and *Jazz UK* magazines in recent years. He was awarded Jazz Instrumentalist of the Year at the 2014 Parliamentary Jazz Awards .Ghosh is a prolific composer, working primarily in the world of theatre and dance. He has worked on over forty professional productions with companies including Manchester Royal Exchange, Library Theatre, National Youth Theatre, Cardboard Citizens, Akademi Dance and Kali Theatre. Ghosh is an Associate Artist of the Albany Theatre and Spitalfields Music (2014), and recently completed his post as Musician in Residence of Wuhan, China in association with the British Council. He first worked with Tamasha as composer on *Child of the Divide* in 2006 and more recently as composer on the verbatim play *My Name is . . .* in 2014.

KITTY WINTER | Movement Director

Kitty Winter is a movement director, choreographer and director. She trained at Laban and on the MA Movement course at the Central School of Speech and Drama. Recent movement credits include: *A Christmas Carol* and *The Rise and Fall of Little Voice* (Derby Theatre); *The Kite Runner, Rapunzel* and *Jack* (Nottingham Playhouse); *Tiny Treasures* and *The Night Pirates* (Theatre Hullabaloo); *The Dog House, Women on the Verge of HRT* and *Puss in Boots* (Derby LIVE). Recent directing credits include: *Feet First* and *Car Story* (Box Clever Theatre); *Spinning Yarns* and *FIVE* (Theatre Hullabaloo/Theatre Direct, Canada); *The Blue Moon* (Wriggle Dance Theatre); *Anything to Declare?* (The Gramophones); *Whose Shoes?* (Nottingham Playhouse); *Awaking Durga* (Kali Theatre/ Soho Theatre). Kitty is Co-Artistic Director of physical theatre company WinterWalker, and has recently produced and directed *Three Keepers* (Déda, Derby/tour) and *The Beast of Belper* (Belper Arts Festival). www.kittywinter.com

RYAN HARSTON | Assistant Director

Ryan Harston is a multi-award-winning creative artist and also the director of URBAN conceptz Theatre. He has worked internationally for the last thirteen years with such companies as Cirque du Soleil, Wired Aerial Theatre and Breaking Cycles. Since making the transition from mid-career performer to emerging director in 2014 he has created and directed shows for a variety of companies including CAST, Breakin' Convention, Freedom Festival Hull and Z-Arts. He is now working with Manchester International Festival, HOME and CAST, where he is Associate Artist. www.uctheatre.co.uk

LAURA STEVENS | Technical Stage Manager

Laura graduated with a First Class Degree in Stage Management in 2010 from Rose Bruford College. Since then she has worked as a freelance stage manager/ CSM and DSM for various production companies. Her recent credits include *Big Sean, Mikey and Me* (Vault Festival, London); *Aladdin* (Watersmeet for PHA); *My Name is . . .* (Arcola Theatre, national tour for Tamasha); *Havana Rakatan* (international tour for Sadler's Wells); *Sampled, Breaking Convention, Zoo Nation Unplugged* (Sadler's Wells); *Little Universe* (Various for Fevered Sleep); *Brown Bomber* (Lillian Baylis Studio/Queen Elizabeth Hall for HMDT); *My Favorite Year* (Bridewell Theatre for LSMT). Laura has also crewed for various companies including Sadler's Wells (Islington), Beck Theatre (Hayes), Pleasance London, Garden Opera, Harlequin Theatre (Redhill), Theatre in the Mill (Bradford) and Gilded Balloon (Edinburgh Festival 2011–2014).

JANE ANDREWS | Company Stage Manager

Jane Andrews trained in Stage Management at the Royal Welsh College of Music and Drama in 2002. Since college, she has worked continuously in stage management for a wide variety of companies, including Opera North, Aldeburgh Music, Birmingham Opera Company, Theatr Clwyd, Salisbury Playhouse, West Yorkshire Playhouse, Filament Theatre, Open Heart Productions, and in 2014 on Tamasha's production of *My Name is . . .*

Cast

KRUPA PATTANI | Caneze

Krupa trained at Drama Studio London. Theatre credits include: *Peter Pan* (Polka Theatre); *Robin Hood* (Octagon Theatre, Bolton); *A Midsummer Night's Dream*, *Othello*, *Cyrano de Bergerac*, *Twelfth Night*, *Masters Are You Mad* (Grosvenor Park Open Air Theatre); *Bollywood Cinderella*, *Kanjoos the Miser*, *Dick Whittington Goes Bollywood* (Tara Arts); *Dinnerladies: Second Helpings* (UK tour); and *Moonfleece* (London and UK tour). TV credits include: *MI High* (Kudos) and *Casualty* (BBC). Film credits include: *Dumpee* (Sasha Collington), *Honeycomb Lodge* (Lesley Manning), *Sick* (NFTS, David Winstone) and *Smoke* (Tuppence Films, Martin Gooch).

ADAM SAMUEL-BAL | Sully

Adam is a graduate of the Guildford School of Acting. Theatre credits include: *Sohovik*, *Damn Yankees* (Brockley Jack); *Aladdin* (Theatre Royal, Leamington Spa); *Half 'n' Half* (National Theatre of Wales); *Children of Eden* (Aria-Entertainment). Workshops include: *Feelin' in the Mood* (Chet Walker) and *Romance of the Rose* (Racky Plews). Commercials include: *AirTel* (Asia).

Blood

Miggy Angel

for justice

Characters

Caneze
Sully

Notes

The words spoken in Mirpuri-Punjabi are not translated within the dialogue but a Glossary is included. The Mirpuri-Punjabi is spoken with ease and mixed together by the characters with English.

A slash (/) in the text indicates an interruption and overlap in the dialogue.

Prologue

Now.

Caneze *is holding a bag full of clothes.*

Sully
  you going?

Caneze
  juss wanna see my Amma, Carly, my friends

Sully
  here then

She stops at the door.

  take this

He gives her his jacket.

  take the mobile
  it's dark

As she opens the door . . .

Sully
  / I need to know you're safe, Caneze . . .

Caneze *suddenly stops in her tracks.*

Caneze
  we're all we got isn't it, Sully?

Beat.

Returns to **Sully**, *hugs him tight.*

Silence.

Sully
  can't deal with it, Caneze
  it's like you don't trust me

He leaves her tight embrace and makes to exit.

Direct address.

Caneze
it's juss my
flesh and blood
my own flesh and blood
it doesn't make sense
if I cut it and it bleeds
it makes sense
I half expect it not to bleed

Sully
cuts me up when she's like this
doesn't know what she means to me

Caneze
. . . juss bickering all the time
sounding like them seagulls that wake me up at four every
morning
how does anyone ever get used to that?

Sully
peoples have different worlds they step in and step out of
and I is no different, I can step into a different world . . .

logical if you think about it

Caneze
. . . got to get out of this shithole
in this godforsaken back o' beyond
never thought I'd end up like this, proper downgraded
been too scared to hang our clothes, just in case

Sully
logical don't mean nish though is it?
family int something you can step into and out of

Caneze

it's everything we been through

Sully

it's after everything we been through
can't blow it

Caneze

can't blow it now
maybe, if we remember what we been through, gotta keep
reminding ourselves – myself

Sully

maybe, if we remember what we been through, gotta keep
reminding ourselves – myself

He returns to her.

One

A year earlier. College canteen.

Direct address.

Caneze

boring shit day doing boring things in this boring college
canteen with people who just go on about things no one
cares 'bout with their dead eye looks thinking they know
everythin and anythin . . .
walking in, I sit with my friends
we're over here and they're over there. it gets worse anyway
cos everyone's got their stupid postcodes now
nobodies eating no food
in this shit stink place with no windows
gawping and checking each other out . . .
Carly, my friend, looking slick in her Republic dress
an' me in me skinny jeans
hair black and my khol green eyes
one-thirty

always late
comes in with the swag
an the swing as if he's somethin
and he says to me:

Sully (*to her*)
jah know where me top dun gone and jah deal with the
teef who teef me tings – dem fe true ere dis!

Direct address.

Caneze
cos I'm wearing his jacket

Beat.

thinks he's funny cos he left it
thinks he's black just gets on
n' I wanna to tell him to shut up and
get to know he ain't no black boy just a proper backwater
Stani

Sully *pulls out a piece of paper and performs his rap to impress her.*

Sully
I got a hunger like no other
and I kinda curious
reach canteen from class
sit broke bombarclart pon bussup seat
in this long-abandoned dungeon
of culinary
fu-ck-ery
put it pon me plate
looking mysterious
smell in the air mek me delirious
is that supposed be chips?
or some dried-up recycled shit
cuisine terrorism bombed

I got a hunger like no other
and I kinda curious
reach canteen from class

wonder what three-shirt-button
ans one dog-eared dinner ticket
gon buy this state-school son
like cancer tumour in this rarseclart carcass
sit broke bombarclart pon bussup seat
in this long abandoned dungeon
of culinary
fu-ck-ery . . .

peace

He looks to **Caneze** *for approval.*

Caneze
   got rhymes
   proper gets carried away tho

Sully (*to her*)
   ahhh sociology man . . . Cath sick lecturer
   the family construct . . . mans that are there for you, look
   out for you . . . here cos o' benefits, hospitals, schools n'
   that it's changed 'the family construct' but that int true
   tho is it? cos where I'm standing, right here, right now,
   its always been tribal, from criminal organisations at
   the top down to the street . . . that makes me laugh 'the
   family construct' . . .

Direct address.

Caneze
   'the family construct' and the world according to Sully . . .

Sully (*to her*)
   wanna come Nando's?

Caneze (*to him*)
   Nando's?!

Sully (*to her*)
   Nando's . . .

Two

Nando's.

Direct address.

Caneze
never been Nando's before . . .

funny going to eat food with some guy
you don't know that well
makes a big difference when
you think it's gonna be some date thing
even though no one has put it across like that
I secretly kinda hope it gets to that

I was that nervous
I got that triple-hot peri-peri sauce whatever it's called
poured it all over my corn on the cob
juss pretended that's how I roll

then
and
then

Beat.

I took a bite . . .

She burns her mouth, fans her hands and gulps her drink.

Sully
/ getting chilli burn – dint think you were some kind of
goree!

Caneze
like I said 'propa backwater Stani'
and then he starts going on like he's the biggest expert
on Nando's . . .

Sully
Nando's man, it's the best, it's halal seen
and their toilets are big n' posh n' smell nice too
an' there's this chicken burger and pittas and even though

I got half a chicken I could get a whole one and there's
all these different types of sauces mild, medium, super-hot
if I want, an' I'm working out the recipe, me being a
chef seen, cos it ain't McDonald's shit like that and . . .

Caneze

/ I'm vegetarian

Sully

vegetarian?!

Caneze

. . . that's why I don't 'know' 'bout Nando's!

Sully

she just sort of sat there looking at me 'Caneze the Veggie'
she didn't really say that much . . .
she seemed quiet y'know peaceful and she made me sort
of stop

Caneze

he looked shocked! I mean proper shook like he'd never
met a veggie before in his life!

Sully (*to her*)

serious – don't like meat?

Caneze (*to him*)

no, don't eat meat . . .

Sully (*to her*)

woah!

Direct address.

Caneze

din't really know what I was doing there with him anyway
think I was just curious
always things you're not supposed to do that
really get you though – isn't it?

Sully

funny that cos the world is so busy, too busy all the time
and everyone's at it

distracted,
texting, facecrapping, pinging
so to just stop n' eat food
with someone who's a vegetarian . . . and doesn't care
was a peaceful, y'know wanna *dem* experiences
deep

then we starts chatting about the fams
I tell her about me brothers runnin travel agents
she liked that innit
knew she would
n' she tells me about her Amma who's ill – that MS –

Caneze
/ my Abba died ten year ago
still ain't over it

Sully
that was sad man

Beat.

and her brother

Caneze (*to him*)
/ y'know Saif Ishak Khan . . .
he sells stuff n' that

Sully (*to her*)
Saif Ishak Khan?!

Caneze (*to him*)
yeah, Saif Ishak Khan
sells designer clothes
and sells stuff like . . . washing powder

Beat.

Direct address.

Sully
SAIF ISHAK FREAKIN KHAN!
that nearly put me off me half a chicken that did –
and nothing puts me off that . . . !

Caneze

    things were going sweet – till then

Sully

    knew then she were a no-go zone
    cos they'd've strung me up by my bollocks cos them lot
    are psychos, gangsters, proper big-time dodgy dealing
    fuckers
    n' if I start telling you 'bout it now
    it's gonna start infecting me right now
    and here I was
    with Saif Ishak Khan's freakin sister

    FUCK!

He smiles nervously at **Caneze**.

    I call you yeah?
    laters . . .

Caneze

    then he juss legged it!

Three

Direct address.

Sully

    din't get in touch after that date
    can't go there, bruv

Checking her mobile for any contact from **Sully**, **Caneze** *receives a text from Carly.*

Caneze

    Carly – so annoying!

    (*Texting back.*) yeah, be there – see you in ten!

    did say he'd call din't he?

maybe he's just ill or somethin
not been at college all week . . .

Sully

big rule in the hood
'do not shit on your own doorstep!'

Caneze

maybe he don't really like me
not really his type or somethin

Sully

brothers preachin: 'trouble the trouble,
then trouble troubles you' true that

Caneze

maybe it's cos I don't love Nando's

Sully

. . . just this hot chick from college wearing me jacket
she really liked me, innit – I could tell

Caneze

might be cos I'm a vegetarian
his face said it all

Sully

conquering me own desires
man can't be weak, innit

Caneze

maybe
cos he made the first move, thinks it's my turn

Sully

fight the temptation . . .

Mobile rings.

SHIT!

it's her . . .

Caneze
meet me?

Sully
where?

Caneze
shisha bar – Desi's – town

Sully
shisha bar – Desi's – town?

Caneze
now!

Sully
cool

Smiles to himself.

Four

Desi's.

Caneze *is sitting.* **Sully** *arrives, stays standing.*

Direct address.

Sully
impressive – wasn't one of dem posh stuck-up bars

Caneze
loading the shisha hubba bubba pipe – it's in the
preparation,
sweet melon to start with, coco-mint for after – got it
planned
flick the lighter – something about fire int there?

Sully (*still standing and nervous*)
don't get me wrong I can hold me own in dem fancy bars,
but, y'know, there's this difference; you feel it
you-know-what-I'm-saying . . .

Caneze *inhales and exhales the shisha pipe, hands it over to him.*

Sully
something about the way she bends the pipe and hands
it over proper but I'm still standing like a numbskull;
I were nervous though and I just went on . . .

(*Nervously to her*) 'love it here, not like them posh bars
is it? they don't want us there do they? them posh bars –
in town – polluting the atmosphere with our poverty –
we're too downgraded'

Caneze
downgraded?
speak for your self!

here . . .
here, Sully
it's about
companionship
who you're sat with
so
first thing you need to do
is sit your freakin ass down

Sully
oh yeah
sit down

He sits.

Caneze
relax

She hands him the pipe again.

They both share the shisha pipe.

Smoke fills the air.

Caneze
you busy later?

Sully
yeah

Caneze
oh

Sully
I can be unbusy though
I mean
change it
I can unchange it
cancel
unbusy it
I mean

Caneze
unbusy yourself?

Sully
straight-up
yeah
cool
for sure
I can – yeah

The chemistry between them is palpable.

Five

Later that night.

Caneze*'s bedroom.*

Sully *at the window.*

Sully
eleven-thirty?

Caneze
on the dot

Sully
    defo not in – yeah?

Caneze
    out by ten-thirty
    truss

Sully
    defo not coming back – no?

Sully
    stays out all night

He climbs into **Caneze**'s *bedroom. She helps him in. He knocks over an ornament.*

Caneze
    shhh . . .

Sully
    where's your Amma?

Caneze
    zonked out – drugs

Sully
    drugs?!

Caneze
    sleeping tabs

Sully
    oh! I thought . . .

A bit stressed, he lights a roll-up and smokes out of the window.

    defo not coming back?

Caneze
    if I have to say it one more time . . .

Sully
    proper sure?

Caneze
sure proper

Sully
quiet round here
loads of trees n' that
your trees seem bigger this ends
and your leaves

He removes a large leaf from his jacket. He finishes his roll-up.

Caneze *moves closer to him.*

He moves closer to her – getting intimate.

your street lighting's brighter
our ends things are dark
it's alright until y'know your . . .

not coming back?

Caneze
can you not bring my big brother into this
puts me off . . .

Sully
. . . can't let *anything* put you off!

Caneze
shhh

Six

Sully *sitting on his own, thinking.*

Sully
not like man like me to be feelin this for one girl
how she can change everythin
juss somethin in the whole world
you know in the whole of the wide
world there's someone there . . . for you
and you, this one particle thing, in the whole wide world
has this other thing, this other tiny particle

and you meet together like that
and you do things together like that
things that other people don't want us to do
and when we do things together, it's proper special – truss
we touch n' we care
and there int that much true care
or touching
in this world
and, it's so hard to be apart
it's like when you're apart
you've left a part of you behind
it's like this seen
love ain't something you just say
just this word
it's something you do
and then you just be
and we just wanna be together
doing things tiogether

Seven

Caneze
and then I blew it

Arguing with her Amma:

he isn't 'just a cook', Amma!
he's a chef – what's wrong with being a cook anyway!
he's a Muslim – like us –
what do you mean he's not 'one of us' . . . ?
I don't need anyone to support me
I know Saif looks after us
I am doing pharmacy
he's studying as well . . .
he's doing sociology
I am grateful to Saif honest, Amma, I am,
I know money doesn't grow on trees

you alright, Amma?
here sit down

Beat.

don't get it

Eight

College canteen

Sully
what's up?

Caneze
you don't want to know

Sully
look
look
can't let pressure get you down

Caneze *is silent.*

Sully
I got a surprise for you

Caneze
not good with surprises, Sully

Sully
two tickets to Sharm . . . Egypt

Caneze
Egypt?!
what about Dubai?

Sully
Dubai?
what's wrong with Egypt?

Caneze
Egypt's dodgy

Sully

Sharm el Sheikh's not – sun, sand, sea,
us – together

Caneze

Dubai's just classier

Beat.

anyways got to keep it on the down low
cos Amma's asking questions . . .

Beat.

Sully

I told you not to say anything, Caneze; you got to keep it
secret like we agreed!

Caneze

don't get it
thought she'd be pleased

and she picked up that text about the coil – what do you
think you were doing?

Sully

fuck!
just when you think it couldn't get worse . . .
defos fucked it now!

Caneze

calm down, I aint a dumb fuck like you,
she din't know it was you; I got your name under Samina

Sully

me name under Samina?
(*Relieved.*) that's slick – my name under Samina – cracks
me up man!
still a bigger dumb fuck though for leaving your mobile
lying around

Caneze

not me leaving me mobile around it's you sending dodgy

texts
where do you get that stupid coil idea from anyway?

Sully

girl at the restaurant

Caneze

what you doing talking to girls at the restaurant about our business?
coils for older peoples; women who've had babies, dumbo!

Sully

/ calm down

Caneze

/ NO, I WON'T CALM DOWN! don't friggin feel calm
could be why she went mad when I told her about you . . .

Sully

it's Saif
he'd have me killed if he found out

Caneze

killed?!
this isn't the friggin *Sopranos* you know!

Sully

shouldn't have told your mum . . .
we agreed

Caneze

she is my mum!
don't get it
proper dumb if you ask me

Sully (*silence*)

Caneze (*silence*)

Sully

could've spent proper time in Egypt
but your Amma knows now

Caneze
/ can't you get your brothers to change tickets to Dubai?

Sully
no – *I* booked it
chop me bollocks off if they knew

Slight pause.

think we shouldn't go?

Caneze
. . . always wanted to go Dubai

Sully
don't agree with it . . .

Caneze
don't agree with what?

Sully
us, sneaking behind people's back like this

Caneze
bit late to be getting righteous

Sully
righteous about what?

Caneze
saying you 'don't agree with it'

(*Upset.*) 'us'

Sully (*reassuring, covering up his previous comment*)
I never said that!

Caneze
just now

Sully
did I?
when?

you juss getting paranoid cos o' your Amma

I don't agree with Dubai
you dundus,
dem Saudis
treated my aunt bad when she got ill at Hajj – man
dropping bars 'bout it – listen . . .

(*Half freestyling.*) I know where de oil man reign
dem count dem blood money
wid dem red right hand
dem a look down pon Indian
and Pakistani man, dem treat ma bredren
and sistren like a third-world problem

now dis sister ere wanna move me desert sides
but me swerve dat request and repeat one time
de Dubai man nah respect me
and me nah respect him
so less juss leave it at that
fore I buss a cap in Arab waste-man
brap, brap, brap!

freestyle!

Caneze

well rubbish
everywhere exploits their workforce, Sully
even friggin Nando's
n' don't get me started on them chickens . . .

She storms off to her lecture.

Sully

what's wrong with Egypt?

no, whatever you do – don't get her started on them
chickens, man . . . used to love Nando's before I met
this girl!

Nine

Caneze
Amma's asking questions sudden
telling me I got to get them A-grades
then Saif starts with: 'don't want you seeing idiots, can't
go university if your knocking 'bout with them idiots'

I knew then Amma and Saif been chatting . . .

Beat.

maybe I am slacking a bit
distracted
they just want me to do well isn't it?
get them A-grades
get the big job
sort everything out
keep it all ticking over nicely

   Slight pause.

if only I could rap about it like Sully does

if only that would sort things

On her laptop she reads and edits her 'rap' as she goes along:

Sully *beat-boxes in the background.*

Caneze
don't know what's got into me
I should study harder

She stops as if trying to block **Sully**'s *'background noise' and starts
again.*

Caneze
don't know what's got into me
I should study harder
so angry with myself

Sully's *beat-boxing starts to creep in.*

Caneze

> don't know what's got into me
> I should study harder
> so angry with myself
> be more conscientious
> get organised
> sort it out
> stay in control
> keep it all ticking over
> nicely

She stops and starts still attempting to block **Sully**'s *'background noise'.*

Caneze

> like I was
> before
> just like my Amma did
> and all my cousins

Sully's *beat-boxing creeps in again.*

Caneze

> be more conscientious
> get organised
> sort it out
> stay in control
> keep it all ticking over
> nicely

Stop, start – as above.

> dreamt about the big career
> car
> house
> home
> husband and kids
> my Amma she nearly had it all
> till my Abba got ill – that is

She stops.

well, that bit rhymes

She starts again and **Sully***'s beat-boxing creeps in as above.*

and I'm doing this for her
studying harder
being more conscientious
getting organised
staying on top

They are finally in harmony.

but do you know what
do you wanna know the truth
deep down
as ironic as it is
and as bad as I feel right now
sometimes, when I'm with Sully I feel strangely free
like this invisible chain is being broken

Ten

Later that night.

Caneze*'s bedroom.*

Stone at the window.

Sully *arrives with plastic plates, Tupperware box of food.*

Stays at the window.

Caneze
din't get my text?

Sully
what text?

He checks his mobile.

soz, forgot to charge my phone!

Caneze

need a break tonight, Sully
got to study . . .

Sully

oh

Beat.

cooked for you . . .

He hands her Tupperware box of food.

Caneze

shhhh
what is it?

Sully

crisp green salad
veggie chasseur . . .

good yeah?

Beat.

I'll juss go

He turns to leave.

Caneze

/ stay

stay Sully

catch up on studies tomorrow morning

Sully *enters.*

Caneze

chasseur supposed to be with chicken and wine isn't it?

Sully

experimenting . . . had to sneak to get wine from
Sainsbury's – avoid Aldi and cheapo shops where biradari
go – get me. got that chicken quorn veggie protein
stuff . . . look here's me recipe . . .

He pulls out his collection of recipes from his pocket and his own handwritten 'adapted' recipe.

Caneze *puts on some music.*

Sully
done some adaptations

Caneze
got loon-march in?

Sully
loon-march?
it's subtle flavours
I'll give you loon-march-ki-bachi!

plenty of thowm though . . . French, innit!

Caneze *lights a candle.*

Caneze
light the candle, all toastie

Sully
aahhh, and a candle, seen . . .
slick team

your Ammee okay is she?

Caneze
good days, bad days – it's hard, sometimes . . .

won't hear a thing, spark out, them temazepams, knocks
her out . . .

Beat.

They unpack and serve the food as if they have done this before.

He hands some to her.

Caneze
gonna end up drunk! only ever been drunk once before –
that Carly the pisshead – who else!

Sully
/ alcohol boils off in cooking
me Amma wondering what the smell was

Caneze
where did you put the bottle?

Sully
like a military operation, poured the drink in an empty
water bottle
left the rest of the bottle with a drunk on the corner

Caneze
should've brought it; could do with getting off my head

Sully
slick team is it – all set up nice for a few hours
Saif out of the way, Ammee off her head

Music continues. They are enjoying themselves.

Caneze
sorry I was going on about Dubai the other day, of course
I'll love Egypt

Sudden sound: **Caneze**'s *mother flushing the toilet . . .*

Sully *and* **Caneze** *stop and freeze.*

Caneze (*whispers*)
lowered her dose – forgot!

and I'm the one who got them to do it

shit!

Sully *makes for the window . . .*

Sully
see you tomorrow

Caneze
shisha bar

Sully
    defo there – shisha bar four o'clock

Caneze
    same spot

They kiss and say their goodbyes as he rushes off.

Eleven

Direct address.

Caneze
    half-term break!

Sully
    Egypt

Caneze
    a whole week of uninterrupted time together

    meeting Sully at the airport – another lie:

    'off to a work placement at Boots Pharmacy, London,
    Amma'

    – and she bought it?!

    hate lying n' I had a bad feeling from the start . . .

Sully
    getting me spices for me holiday with me girl
    loving the smell of me uncle's karahi gosht, outside his
    bakery shop – love it here
    juss cotching, people watching isn't it?

Caneze (*on her mobile*)
    stop, redial, stop, redial, stop, redial, stop

    sat there just doing that for a freaking whole hour . . . and
    then another hour, anyone with any sense would've
    moved on, but I lost all sense

Sully

    when this car screeches in front of me, I was surrounded
    by, I think, 'bout five men, one wore this green t-shirt
    the others wore suits

Caneze

    it all just became this blur, next minute I looked up we'd
    missed the flight . . . just sat there feeling a proper idiot
    sat at Heathrow passenger lounge with my friggin luggage
    on me raas worst experience ever . . .

Sully

    I was hit three times . . . I think, last killer punch knock
    me down – I fell to the ground, kicked in the ribs,
    kicked in the stomach, marrch and haldi everywhere,
    heard one of them say 'you go near her it'll be her
    kneecaps next'

Caneze

    I knew when he wasn't picking up that something bad
    had happened, I mean, really bad and I started with
    the butterflies . . .

Sully

    waking up in hospital, me mum crying . . . kissing me
    hand, my brothers asking me 'who done it?' I didn't
    speak . . .
    fractured ribs,
    fractured insides
    I stayed wired
    and silenced
    din't I?

Twelve

Caneze (*ringing* **Sully**)

    pick up – Sully – please – please Sully – pick up
    Sully – pick up – please

Sully *is not picking up. He switches his phone off.*

Caneze
    then peeps start chatting big time BS at you . . .

She confronts **Sully**'s *friend.*

Caneze
    stop with the bull crap
    what do you mean his Ba-ji's ill
    think I'm some idiot –
    I know y'not telling the truth
    I know y'not
    tell him
    tell him
    he needs to speak to me – direct
    no one else
    stop sayin he's going to be in touch
    stop with tutti
    tell him to call me direct
    not his friends – not you
    him

Thirteen

Direct address.

Sully (*injured*)
    brothers sorting out tickets
    things taken out of my hands

Caneze
    monkey grinder comes to see me again
    tells me:

    'Sully's gone to a
    family emergency in Pakistan
    he'll tell you more later'

    says 'believe it, Caneze'

believe it!?

believe what?!

a whole month
not a word

Sully
    a month later
    at Heathrow
    instead of terminal two going to Egypt with Neze,
    I was in terminal five – to Pakistan

Fourteen

Caneze (*imitates Saif*)
    'gone back to staniland to get hitched innit' Saif says

    dint 'believe' that

    then he sticks his big fat nose in again
    saying 'that Sully fucked off like the downgraded
    baffoon he is – off to marry some backwater village
    girl – cos that's all boys like him are good for'

    I told him it's a family emergency, 'he'll be back soon,
    I know'

    'is that what he saying? he ain't coming back for real; gone
    off to marry his cousin like the six-toe-fucker he is'

Beat.

    waiting
    and
    waiting
    for a sign
    anything
    text
    wassapp

instagram
anything

then it hit me, it hit me hard like a ten-ton weight –
he's gone, I mean really, gone

Beat.

I juss couldn't move
couldn't get out of bed for over a week
the shock of it!

Fifteen

Sully

'you go near her it'll be her kneecaps next'

Slight pause.

peoples have different worlds they step in and step out of . . .
and I is no different, I can step into a different world
this was one of those times when I defo needed to step
into and out of

logical if you think about it . . .

Sixteen

Caneze *finds the rap she wrote previously and reads.*

'but do you know what
do you wanna know the truth
deep down
as ironic as it is
and as bad as I feel right now
sometimes, when I'm with Sully I feel strangely free
like an invisible chain is being broken'

She shuts her laptop.

my Amma always chants this prayer when she's in pain:

'A'udhu bi 'izzati Allahi wa qudratihi mimma ajidu wa
uhadhir.'

it's about protection from pain

maybe, just maybe, there is something in that,
maybe, if you follow things by the 'book' you wouldn't
hurt so much . . .

*She searches and finds a random 'Islamic' quote on her mobile. She
reads.*

New Age Islam – an Islam for the twenty-first century:
'The Qur'an, however, allows sexual relationship between
a man and a woman only through wedlock and gives
full freedom in this regard – albeit within broader
paradigms of morality'

She puts her headscarf on. Looks in the mirror.

Bismillah ir Rahman ir Raheem

She picks up her prayer beads and chants a prayer

Seventeen

In Pakistan.

Sully
in Pakistan like royalty
paradin round all khandan
it's like they all want a piece of me
feel like I ain't got nothing left to give
shirts from Primark, fake perfume and fraud smiling, innit
pressure to be happy when I aint feeling it – killing me inside

Eighteen

Caneze

Ramzaan time
Amma juss got worse n' ending up in hospital
fasting for her sunrise to sunset
sometimes I didn't eat for days . . .

my brother buying me shit as if buying 'stuff' is gonna fix
it all
Paul Smith coat, designer hijabs . . .
cos that what it says in the Qur'an don't it:
'thou shalt wear a Dolce and Gabbani rip-off . . . '

no, Saif, I'm not police
just wanna know where all this stuff comes from – that's all
no, I don't want to go out with your mates,
just don't fancy it
I'm not interested in Yousuf . . .
I know Amma doesn't think I'm happy
tell her I am happy, just quietly happy
tell her cos she listens to you – *everyone listens to you*

no I don't want to go the mosque like all them other
women . . .
there isn't just one way to Allah like most of the stupid
people round here think

Nineteen

In Pakistan.

Sully

fast-packed action of working in kitchens, working here
in my uncle's travel agents is a totally different scene
having to act all posh n' that,
gets boring, don't get me wrong I got into it, just pace

of life slower here, gives you time to think, three months
since I seen Caneze.

He looks at his mobile.

'her kneecaps next tho'

leave it

He puts his mobile away.

my auntie in the evenings stressing me, on me case, giving
me a whole heap of shit

He imitates his auntie.

'Suleiman! Suleiman! what's the matter with you? what's
boiling away inside your head?
talk to me?'

I'm alright, khala

'no – I want you to look at me and tell me'

. . . it's too hot, gets to me, still not used to . . .

'I was young – one time
I know what it's like'

there's nothing wrong, khala

'you think your khala doesn't know things
I know things
you have to just get on with life, just go hahahaha!
be happy, nothing to worry about, just be happy'
(*She sings.*) 'don't worry, be happy'

'where are you going?'

out
see my friend

Twenty

Caneze

my Amma coming out of hospital for Eid, then she wasn't
right so they readmitted her

Slight pause.

what can you do?

*Checking her mobile and laptop – disappointed as she realises there is
no message from* **Sully**.

Beat.

I say to Saif: Amma'll be upset if she knows your storing
boxes in her room

he juss says, 'I checked it out with her and she's cool, and
that it's you Amma's worried about'

Beat.

then he says: 'you need to socialize with the other women
and girls who go to mosque n' that, specially cos
Amma's sick in hospital'

don't know how many more times I could say this to this
lot but
there *isn't* just one way to Allah like most of the stupid
people round here think . . . !

She chants prayer with her beads.

doing it my own way see

praying for my Amma

then he starts lecturing me . . .

'in Islam it says "paradise is at the sole of your mother's
feet"'

. . . yeah, and?

tells me he's doing right by Amma and how I should meet
his mate cos 'Yousuf is A-grade' and 'Sully is a
downgrade baffoon'

I take no notice

then he really starts puttin the pressure on telling me how
he's gonna marry his girlfriend 'Anastasia' –

I laughed cos I thought that int gonna work, she's just this
Russian money-grabbing whore – and Amma isn't
going to have that . . .

Twenty-One

Sully *pondering with his mobile.*

Sully

time ticking by doesn't get any easier

'trouble the trouble then trouble troubles you'
true that

Beat.

Puts his mobile down.

Caneze *sitting waiting for a text, call, anything.*

Sully

my auntie uppin the pressure

Imitating his auntie:

'need you to come and help fix my friend's gate'

you really need me, khala? I seen you fix that door last
week

'I'm just a frail old woman'

you make the best khanna in the world – no one that frail
does that –
believe, that's a super power you got there . . .

'you flatter me – now my friend's gate'

yeah, this gate . . .

off to 'fix' this gate knowing full well my auntie was
chatting bare tutti I'd end up visiting some family with
some girl, and ten cups of chai later I'd finally manage
to escape realizing there was no gate to fix, just me and
this girl – get me? it were like practising kung-fu
self-defence trying to deflect all my auntie's scheming
in that department

Twenty-Two

Caneze

. . . and you never guess what, you freakin never guess
what! this Anastasia, this random money-grabber whore
from back o' beyond goes and converts to Islam like a
proper big-time batty licker, innit!

then she goes and changes her name to freakin Khadija
Maryam – went from a designer-wearing slapper to
niqab-wearing ninja overnight!

competing with me all the time – looking over me shoulder
when I'm praying – I was praying for myself, not for
anyone else's benefit – can't they get that into their
thick brains round here . . .

Twenty-Three

Sully

winter now, not like winter in England, winter here is like
summer in England – yanno cold!

Slight pause.

> this girl me auntie was trying to fix me up with thought
> I'd juss give it go, thought it'd help me forget

Beat.

> but, y'know not my type – y'know guys when you think
> you're the one who needs to wear one of them niqabs –
> know what I'm saying . . .

> juss made me think of Caneze

> only thing keeping me okay was reading the poems – my
> uncle a big fan of that that poet Faiz Ahmed Faiz –
> lovin that Faiz . . .

He reads from 'A Prison Evening' by Faiz Ahmed Faiz.

> could read shit like that anywhere
> and I know I'd be home.
> wish they taught you about situations like this in school!

> > 'On the roof, the moon – lovingly, generously is
> > turning the stars into a dust of sheen.'

He continues reading aloud, looks up at the stars.

> bigger things up there int there, the sun, the moon
> and stars
> you ever get that feelin when you just wanna howl at
> the moon

He shouts at the sky, shouting the final lines of the poem.

> that's true
> cos I know she'll finish her college
> she'll go to uni isn't it
> like she always talked about it
> that's when she'll be away from that idiot psycho brother
> and those thugs
> I'll go and find her then – seen

Twenty-Four

Caneze *throws her old mobile in the bin. Opens a new box, with her new fancy phone.*

Caneze
    Saif got me this:
    upgrade newest model

    new number; fresh start

    Amma's much better now and out of hospital. telling me
    to just meet with Yousuf cos 'Yousuf is A-grade' and
    'paradise is at the sole of your mother's feet' isn't it?
    so I did, no real harm in it – is there? just to meet –
    once – is there? make Amma happy . . .

(*To Yousuf.*) y'know, Yousuf
    she isn't true in her heart this Khadija Maryam is she?
    proper devious . . . can't believe Saif and my Amma
    are taken in
    then Yousuf said:

    'we should go out again, accompanied. do everything by
    the book cos that's the only way to alleviate the
    suffering and stay close to Allah, innit!'

    we both talked about getting away from here. it was like
    he could read my mind cos I was dying to get away
    from here, just with Amma's blessing, and she likes
    Yousuf. he said I could maybe pick up on my studies
    next year, after we travelled

    getting my life back on track, yeah? don't know what I ever
    saw in Sully the user, village idiot low-life – running
    back like the dumbass that he is . . .

Twenty-Five

Sully *listens and sings along to the radio. Looking at his watch.*

Sully (*imitating a usual phone call*)
'Good afternoon Mai Ikra travel sai phone kurra-hu I got
you a 6.30 a.m. flight from Karachi Airport to Chicago
USA arriving at 23.15 Amreeka time, teek hey? bas.
goodbye.'

well no one would've understood if I say: 'that flight from
Karachi is kinda cheap tings yanno, in fact bare cheap
for your extras, innit fam?'

Slight pause.

when I'm really bored I go on a stalkbook spying on peeps
back in England – don't tell me you haven't done it,
spied on your ex to see what they been doin see if they
friending new man n' shit, that's all stalkbooks about
isn't it. using Carly's password, cos she unfriended,
I sign in. I knew she'd kinda gone all religious veiled up
n' that, but today, today, things were different . . .

(*Disgusted.*) booked me return flight there and then . . .

THIS IS FUCKED UP SHIT, MAN!

Twenty-Six

Sound of a stone thrown at Caneze's window.

Slight Pause

Sully
Caneze

Beat.

Caneze looks out of the window.

Caneze
go away

Sully
I'm sorry

Slight pause.

Caneze
  (*Beat.*)

Sully
  need to see you
  this once
  please
  let me in

Caneze
  Sully, its over

Sully
  don't make me beg like this
  truss
  one chance
  karane kasme . . .
  Caneze
  c'mon

He climbs through the window

Caneze
  stay there!

Beat.

Sully
  been time since I sneaked in here

  love the curtains
  see they finally fixed that pipe

  looking good, you're looking good

Caneze
  things change Sully – everything changes

Slight pause.

Obvious tension.

Sully *attempts to move towards* **Caneze**.

Caneze
  stay there!

Sully (*trying to lighten the mood*)
  reminds me of school, standing in the corner like this you
  want me to face the wall like they used to make you

He laughs nervously.

  raah they'd *always* make me stand in the corner,
  that Ms Strelly always picking on me. man, still ain't
  over it, she'd make me stand in the corner away from
  everyone else . . .

Slight pause.

Awkward atmosphere.

  I was six. I just stood there, looking at the magazines,
  she'd bring in for the class, cut up and do pictures, with
  glue, like they used to – remember?

Slight pause.

  I loved those pictures, you know the recipes
  'how to make a chicken chasseur'
  I was six and I learnt to read and write like that
  I learnt (*He spells it out.*) 'c-h-a-s-s-e-u-r'

Caneze
  never grow up, still chatting the same bullshit

Sully
  raah French cooking got wine innit
  remember me buying wine like a military operation

Caneze
  what do you want, Sully?

Sully
  if you come with me I'll do you that veggie chasseur

Caneze
  don't drink the piss

Sully
> don't say that, Caneze: I never drunk no piss in cooking
> all the alcohol boils off, they wouldn't say it at the
> mosque, but in here my heart's clean; Allah knows my
> heart's clean and that's all that matters . . .
>
> still love those pictures I've got a good collection of recipes
> now from Pakistan

He moves – **Caneze** *wrongly assuming it's for her. She moves away.*

Sully
> want a smoke, Neze – twos-up?

She glares at him.

Sully (*lights a cig*)
> always love it round here – the peace
> you lot got a monopoly on great views
> and peace
> you buy it don't you
> so you own it

Caneze
> 'you lot'?!

Sully
> Mughals

Caneze
> don't come back spouting your backwater clan shite!

Sully
> but that's what it's all about in the end isn't it?
> fam, the clan, sticking together

Caneze
> if you haven't got family what have you got, starts with
> family, ends with family,
> family in the middle, blood is thicker than water

Sully *shakes his head.*

Caneze
> me and Yousuf are getting a flat in the city centre

might go travelling before we settle down, thinking of
going to Dubai

Sully

Dubai?!

He laughs in disbelief.

Caneze

being with the people that care about me makes me happy

Sully

you're not like them, Yousuf and Saif, you got to believe,
Caneze
you're like me

Caneze

come all this way to just slag my brother and fiancé off –
joke, Sully

fucked off without freakin a word

Sully

had to leave they would've killed me;
brothers got me out

Caneze

same old shit, never grow up, Sully
better go everyone'll be back soon

Sully

if they come back, I'll disappear into the cracks
good at that

Caneze

say you broke in – that's the truth . . .

Sully

I'm not a criminal, Caneze, what have I ever done?
nothing – fuck all

Caneze

loser – that sound better

Sully

good brainwashing job done on you

Caneze

no one's done a job on me, Sully

Sully

they said they'd hurt you too
dint want them to hurt you
I know what they can do
he's got contacts your brother

Caneze

/ Saif would never hurt me, I'm his sister
just does what he's got to do to look after his family
that is all
you could do with taking a leaf out of his book
starts with family, ends with family, family in the middle

Sully

blood is thicker than water – heard you the first time

Caneze

you believe that too:
your brothers tell you to jump, you just say how high
right Mirpuri biradari caveman system you got going
on there
proper common
piss off out of the friggin country cos they say
not even out of the country
you left the fuckin continent
not a word
nothing
you could've got in touch once

Sully

they beat me up
put me in hospital, Caneze

Beat.

She shakes her head.

I thought it was for the best
believe, Caneze
they said they hurt you dint want them to hurt you
I'd come back when things died down . . . when you go
uni – dint think you were juss gonna go and marry one
of them thugs . . .

Caneze

believe?!
believe?!
sick of people telling me what to believe
you don't know the meaning of the word
not your business, Sully, what I do and don't do

Sully

they're dangerous guys

Silence.

Caneze

he's my brother – they look out for me –
Saif – and Yousuf – my Amma's known Yousuf from time
know where he's coming from
you – just cos you've messed your life up
don't come back here and do this to mine
they're here; you wasn't
actions speak louder, Sully

Slight pause.

Sully

I been reading them Sufi poets, from back home, make
you look at things different, here's Bulleh Shah

He hands her the book. She doesn't take it. He leaves it on her table.

you should read it, Caneze; love to read you some Rumi
listen to Abida Parveen; cook you veggie chasseur, we
never gave ourselves that chance did we?

Caneze

  had veggie chasseur, didn't work, chasseur only works
  with dead meat!

Doorbell rings.

Caneze (*to* **Sully**)

  quick!

Sully

  got my job back at Shimla's, you need anything, you know
  where I am – I mean anything, Caneze

He exits.

Twenty-Seven

Caneze

  doorbell ringing
  an' I weren't expecting no one
  when I saw him at the front door, Yousuf, I should've
  known better than to let him in, he shouldn't have
  been here and I knew it weren't right but sometimes
  it's hard to say no to some peoples

She retells the story of Yousuf.

  he said:

  'I come to see you
  I'm sorry I shouldn't come round like this
  I know it's wrong, I know
  but I just got to see you

  look, I wanted to ask you something
  it's your birthday next week right

  oh
  sorry I missed it
  I wanted to propose properly, sort of on your birthday
  though . . . '

will you marry me?
I know, but I never done this – have I?
look, I got this magazine
Asian Bride, you read it

could ask for something better
a better venue for the wedding,
we could hire the castle in town

we could have a big party there after the wedding
and write our story in the magazine
look at this . . .

Fozia and Alif made in heaven

"we soon started to look for a suitable venue for the
wedding and decided on the Empire Banqueting Suite"

look at the pictures

why not?
we can afford it
it'll be brilliant
we can hire two bands and a DJ
we could arrive in a helicopter

what's wrong with showing off
cos it's always been about showing your money,
if you can't do it on your wedding day when can you do it
doesn't matter where you come from

you got your dress right?
look this guy here made sure his suit matched his bride's
dress
at our party, at the castle
that's when we could . . .
listen to this
Ravi had co-ordinated the colour scheme of my outfit
with the venue's décor. Ravi wore a matching designer
sherwani
and later changed into his Armani suit . . . "

we're getting married
it's all ok,
we're going to spend the rest of our lives together

you'll be all mine soon
everything about you will belong to me

I don't know why you're scared
I'm going to be your husband
it really makes no difference

you should be aching for me

why you playing righteous
little miss shy virgin
don't think I don't know
what you got up to before it got sorted

I know
I don't listen to them rumours
cos you're mine; have always been there
for me, and no one else would touch you, come near you,
not after you been sullied by one of them low-downs
if anyone of them come anywhere near you again
he'd be killed

I'm going to be your husband
and what do you think your mother's going to do
she's my best "auntie" isn't she?
she wouldn't mind me here
treats me like I'm one of her own
special
Saif knows I'm here
I could give you something if you want
a little something to make you feel better
look, don't look worried
I don't mean to frighten you

Beat.

no need to say anything about my visit'

Slight pause.

> I should've fought, but I didn't, he ripped my dress and
> kept on

Beat.

> couldn't tell a soul

Beat.

> I tried

Beat.

> but

Twenty-Eight

Slight pause.

Caneze *takes out her wedding outfit, bangles etc. Looks at them.*
Thinks. Then quickly grabs her jeans, tops and knickers, throws stuff
in a bag – her laptop, and leaves.

Twenty-Nine

Caneze *meets* **Sully**. *He has a weapon.*

Sully
> you've got to tell me
> I'll keep looking
> up and down these streets
> I know this town from time
> been here all me life
> I'll find him

Caneze
> he's with Saif

Sully
>he did this
>just him, Yousuf
>one on one

Caneze
>not just Yousuf, Saif knew, they all knew
>my Amma . . .

She walks to leave. **Sully** *stays standing.*

Beat.

Caneze
>you can't fight them, Sully
>not on your own
>where are your brothers then?
>where are they now?
>
>. . . I got to go, Sully
>. . . we got to get away

Beat.

Sully
>what you got?

Caneze
>knickers, few clothes

Sully
>mobile?

She nods.

>give me

He takes out the SIM.

>this is hassle

He breaks it in half and throws it away.

Caneze
>Skegness – next train

Sully

    peeps I know go Skeggy

Caneze

    do they?

Sully *nods.*

Sully

    next?

Caneze

    don't know – Cleethorpes, Grimsby, it says . . .

Sully

    how long?

Caneze

    seven mins

Sully

    come – quick!

They leave.

Thirty

Later. Sitting by the beach.

Caneze

    funny, been in England all my life and still feel as if I've
    come off a boat or something

    see how she looked at me when I told her I were vegetarian

Sully

    yeah, noticed that

Caneze

    anyways, you nearly ended up veggie after I'd finished
    with you

Sully

. . . stopped eating as much meat
dint eat that much meat in Pakistan
don't have a kebab shop on every corner

Caneze

and a Nando's on every high street

Sully

give it time
kill for a Nando's now

Caneze

she looked at me like 'beggars can't be choosers'
suppose beggars can't be choosers

Sully

could go somewhere else
don't have to go soup kitchens for food

Caneze

got to ain't we, only so much money left . . . today's
deposit . . . month's rent in advance . . . daren't use my
credit card

Sully

look for work tomorrow; it's gonna be alright
just gotta believe its gonna work out

Caneze

work out?
no evidence in my life of anything working out, Sully

Sully

could go police

Caneze

police?
and say what?

Sully

whole story
that they'll kill us

Beat.

Caneze

Saif's got friends in high places, truss, me and Amma
had to make chai and samosa for the police chief at
our house once . . .

Sully

sorry I left when I did

Caneze

dint have a choice did you – know that now

Sully

do have a choice, Caneze – know that now
they say 'don't shit on your own doorstep'
'don't trouble the trouble'
that's juss bullshit
serious bullshit
shits here already, everywhere, in the house, on the
doorstep, street,
top to the bottom
juss no one gonna clear it – that's the problem

The sound of a church clock chiming.

Caneze

nice of that church I suppose, when she said do I want to
light a candle for Jesus? Jesus was a prophet of Allah,
wasn't he?
so I lit that candle

Sully

not sure about
'the incarnation of God's eternal Son, the Lord Jesus Christ'

Caneze

that's what they believe though isn't it?

Sully

want you to believe what they believe –
that's the issue with most peoples
wanting you to believe what they believe

she couldn't wait to get her claws into you when you lit
that candle . . .

Caneze

. . . not sure what I believe any more

Sully

I believe in us

don't you?

She nods.

Sully

he can't get to us now . . .

Caneze

don't want to keep going back to that soup kitchen; have
to proper swallow your pride, every time you go back
reminds you how shit things are

Sully

we got each other now that's what matters
no more sneaking; no more secrets or lies

Caneze

no more secrets, no more lies
except our whereabouts
that's a big fat lie

Sully

remember what I told you, Caneze
'they cannot snuff out the moon'
at the end of the day that's all
that's left now
and at the end of the day that's what matters

look
look out there
look
see how vast it is
there's room for everyone
don't know why we're fighting all the time

waste of friggin time
sometimes I look at the moon
for safety
show me the way
and sometimes I'm waiting for the sun
for morning
and do you know what
the moon is there
and then the sun is there
they're not gonna let me down
or fuck with me head
they promised
from the beginning of time
that they're gonna be there
and they have been there
haven't they?
it's important to remember that
that there's bigger things out there
that don't let you down
promise me you won't forget that
no matter what happens . . .

Thirty-One

Caneze *in their new flat. Writing a letter, on her laptop, to her mother.*

Dear Amma

I'm so sorry, really I am
I'm not bad, really I'm not
I'm sorry things have worked out the way they have
I know how upset you'll be
and I just want you to know that I dint want it to be this way
it's not my fault
I wanted to do the right thing
I'm sorry

> sorry
> sorry

Sully *returns with some basic supplies. Walks straight in and startles her. She shuts the laptop, hiding the letter, as he bolts the door.*

Sully
> keep it bolted . . . just in case

Caneze
> doorbell doesn't work
> need a knock
> a code – so we know it's us

She does a coded knock. Like a heartbeat – four beats.

Sully *repeats with three beats.*

Caneze (*repeating the knock*)
> four beats remember

Sully *and* **Caneze** (*in unison*)
> our knock

Caneze
> scary shit this! should get a gun, shoot him if he ever
> come near me again

Sully
> guns cost money . . .
> about eight Indian restaurants in this place; someone'll
> take some cash-in-hand work

Caneze
> maybe there'll be job in a chemist and then
> maybe I could enrol at the college and start me
> training again get life back on track

Thirty-Two

Direct address.

Sully

from this day on everything became about trust

Caneze

dint get a job in a chemist, ended up in a pub, in the
kitchens, the boss tried to get me to work on the bar in
a short skirt, but I managed to swerve that one . . . long
story. told people I was Jamaican mixed Brazilian,
could've said anything to this lot dint matter who I was,
just who I wasn't and I wasn't one of them that was sure.

Sully

I were giving a false name
I were looking for people
who wouldn't question, know what I mean
on me seventh try
I found a restaurant willing to give me work
who dint ask questions
willing to buy into the cover in exchange for cheap labour

Caneze

covered that nasty wallpaper with pictures bought new
fresh bedding
that was the first thing I got

couldn't wait for Sully to come home

Sully

had to sign on, dint want to, dint want to put our address
on any official record, dint trust Saif and his
connections, dint really have a choice needed the
money. then one night in the restaurant, one Saturday
night, there were a bit trouble from some pissheads . . .
I got meself out on the front to help; they dint even
have to ask cos I knew the score, been there before
ain't I? whole thing got sorted pretty quick, relieve man!
everyone were different with me after that, things

changed – a bit, seemed to have a bit more respect,
they even let me do a bit a cooking; helping the chef n'
that. that was well boss and things were beginning to
look up –

a bit

Thirty-Three

Caneze *is continuing her letter on her laptop.*

Sully *knocks – coded knock.*

She hides the letter, then unbolts amd lets **Sully** *in.*

He has a carrier bag full of food.

Sully
Hugh Fearnley-Whittingstall, proper bo!

*He takes out the torn recipe from a magazine, unfolds it to show
to* **Caneze**.

Caneze
sad

Sully *(kissing it)*
look at that pic, me and you are going to have this tonight –
'fried houllumi salad
with paprika' – yum!

He puts the music on and starts to cook.

Caneze *switches it off.*

Caneze
don't like that racket

Sully
the racket's out there, that traffic, this covers that racket up

He switches it on. She switches it off.

Caneze
don't add to it with more noise

Beat.

how much did all this cost you anyway?

Sully
don't ask . . .

Caneze
we can't afford it

Sully
just one little treat that is all

Caneze
nothing feels a treat in this stinky place

Sully
plug in that Glade freshener thing

Caneze
can't afford the leccy

Sully
for fuck's sake, Caneze
gonna get some of them agar-bathis tomorrow

He goes to plug in the Glade and switches the music on.

Caneze *switches the music off and unplugs the 'Glade'.*

Sully *stops. He looks at her.*

Sully
not in the mood for this today, Caneze, not again, I can't
deal with it

He leaves and slams the door.

Caneze *reads her letter.*

Caneze
Dear Amma,
I hate you for taking Saif's blood money

I hate that he thinks he can do what he wants
I hate that you don't question it
I hate you for not really listening to me
thinking about me
I hate that you put what other people think above what
I think or feel
I hate that . . .

She attempts to rap – as in Scene Nine.

don't know what's got into me
I should be stronger

Stops.

don't know what's got into me
and I'm so angry with myself
I should be stronger
be more conscientious
get organised
sort it out

Stops.

stay in control
keep it all ticking over nicely
don't know
don't know what's got into me
I should be stronger
be more conscientious
get organised
sort it out
stay in control
keep
keep it
ticking over nicely

*She goes to where **Sully** has been cooking, takes a knife and harms herself.*

Sully *returns.*

She bleeds.

Sully *sees* **Caneze** *cutting herself – and the blood.*

Sully
  Neze, what are you doing?!

Caneze *puts down the knife.*

Caneze
  juss read that it supposed to make you feel better

Sully *wipes the blood, covers the wound.*

Sully
  did it make you feel better?

Caneze
  no

  it's juss my
  flesh and blood
  my own flesh and blood
  it doesn't make sense
  if I cut it and it bleeds
  it makes sense
  I half expect it not to bleed

  blood supposed to be thicker than water isn't it?

Sully
  can't punish yourself like this

Caneze
  I'm their flesh and blood

Sully
  I know

He holds out the mobile for her. She doesn't take it.

Sully
  you want to report him?

Caneze
  who to

Sully
  different police here

Caneze (*silence*)

Sully *is still holding the mobile.*

Sully
  can't carry on like this

Caneze (*silence*)

Sully
  can't go over and over this from time – you got to get out
  of this place

Caneze
  I would – if I had an alright place to work – like you
  you got them friends

Sully
  your friends too

Caneze
  no one likes me in that rancid kitchen I work
  I hate them too
  maybe best to just go back

She takes her bag that has her stuff and goes towards the door.

Sully *doesn't believe her.*

Sully
  you going?

Caneze
  juss wanna see my Amma, Carly, my friends

Sully
  here then

Caneze *stops at the door.*

Sully
    take this

He gives her his jacket.

    take the mobile
    it's dark

As she opens the door . . .

Sully
    / I need to know you're safe, Caneze . . .

She stops in her tracks.

Caneze
    we're all we got isn't it, Sully?

Beat. Returns to **Sully***, hugs him tight.*

Silence.

Sully *hugs her back*

    can't deal with it, Caneze
    it's like you don't trust me

Caneze
    maybe, if we remember what we been through, gotta keep
    reminding ourselves – myself

Sully
    maybe, if we remember what we been through, gotta keep
    reminding ourselves – myself

Caneze *leaves his embrace and reads out her letter to* **Sully***. He
listens.*

Caneze
    Dear Amma,
    I hate you for taking Saif's blood money
    I hate that he thinks he can do what he wants
    I hate that you don't question it
    I hate you for not really listening to me
    thinking about me

I hate that you put what other people think above what
I think or feel
I hate that . . .
I hate that you and everyone listen to Saif
cos
cos
it's easy
and he buys your affections
and everyone else's
and you let him
and I hate that you look down on other people
Yousuf came to visit me under your roof
and he hurt me
bad
really bad

that's how much he really likes me
how does that make you feel
under your roof
that's how much real respect he has for you
and I hate him for what he did to me
and what he's doing to you
and I hate you because you're too fuckin stupid
but I know you're not stupid, Amma
you just don't see . . .
n' I hate you for choosing not to see

Sully *takes the laptop. Puts it away.*

(*Freestyle.*) blood is thicker than water . . .

Caneze
love is thicker than blood

Sully
blood can't exist without water

Caneze
water can exist without blood

Sully

like it: water *can* exist without blood

y'know this one: 'blood makes relatives'

Caneze

love makes family

Sully

and I'm your family now
going to cook for you, Caneze, it'll be good.

*He switches the music on and carries on cooking. Music: ' Laal:
Umeed-e-Sahaar' by Faiz Ahmed Faiz.*

Caneze *goes to the bin liners where they have their clothes. She starts
to hang up their clothes.*

Sully

thought you said they're best in bin liners,
just in case we got to run –
do one of our fast getaways

Caneze

comes a point, had enough of bin liners and bags, Sully

*The music swells as she makes further changes to transform the flat into
their home.*

Thirty-Four

Next evening.

Caneze *is reading* **Sully***'s Sufi poetry book.*

Sully *knocks.*

Caneze *lets him in. She has been looking forward to him coming
home.*

He enters with shopping.

Sully

I got the agar bathis – the incense – y'know
ain't going to waste the leccy

not going to play the music – if you don't want

here I'll light one

He lights the incense.

Caneze

there's something about fire in there?

Sully

you haven't hurt yourself again – no?

don't feel right about leaving you on your own

I rang rape crisis they were good

Caneze

you did?

Sully

sorry – I didn't say anything but I just didn't know what
to do after you hurt yourself –
they won't talk to me,
they need you to call
gave me numbers for other services, I rang but there's
 waiting lists

He leaves their shared mobile on the table.

here have the this tomorrow when I'm out
do you want me to get someone to stay with you?
one of the guys at work he's got daughters they're really
good . . .

Caneze *looks at the mobile.*

Caneze

/ stop talking Sully

*She attempts to kiss him. There is a sound outside as if somebody is
there – bins crashing or something – they both stop.*

Suddenly terrified..

She grabs the kitchen knife and holds it. **Sully** *grabs something that could be used as a weapon.*

He goes to look.

Returns.

Sully
just the wind

Relieved.

They embrace.

The End.

Glossary

Abba	Father
Agar-bathis	Incense sticks
Amma	Mother
Ba-ji	Grandfather (affectionate)
Biradari	Patrilineal kin
Chai	Tea
Goree	White woman
Haldi	Tumeric
Karahi gosht	Spicy stir-fry lamb
Khala	Auntie (mother's sister)
Khandan	Family
Khanna	Dinner
Loon	Salt
Marrch	Chilli
Mirpuri	Someone who originates from Mirpur, Azad Kashmir
Mughals	A clan
Ramazan	The holy month of Ramadan
Sherwani	Long coat-like garment closed up to the neck, worn by men in India and Pakistan
Thowm	Garlic
Tutti	Diarrhoea

Amreeka time, teek hey?
  America time, is that okay?
A`udhu bi `izzati Allahi wa qudratihi mimma ajidu wa uhadhir
  I seek refuge and protection in the august might and power
  of Allah from the pain and illness I am suffering from and
  I am afraid of (Ibn Majah)
Bismillah ir Rahman ir Raheem
  Allah the most beneficent the most merciful
Loon-marrch-ki-bachi
  Daughter of salt and chilli (an affectionate tease)
Sai phone kurra-hu